WITCHES AND WITCHCRAFT

David Nash

SHIRE PUBLICATIONS

SHIRE PUBLICATIONS
Bloomsbury Publishing Plc

Kemp House, Chawley Park, Oxford OX2 9PH, UK
29 Earlsfort Terrace, Dublin 2, Ireland
1385 Broadway, 5th Floor, New York, NY 10018, USA
Email: shire@bloomsbury.com
www.shirebooks.co.uk

SHIRE is a trademark of Osprey Publishing Ltd

First published in Great Britain in 2014
Transferred to digital print in 2023

A catalogue record for this book is available from the
British Library.

Shire Library no. 765
Print ISBN: 978 0 74781 291 3
ePDF: 978 0 74781 535 8
ePub: 978 0 74781 534 1

Designed by Tony Trucott Designs, Sussex, UK
Typeset in Perpetua and Gill Sans
Printed and bound in India by Replika Press Private Ltd.

24 25 26 27 28   15 14 13 12 11 10

COVER IMAGE
Matthew Hopkins, Witch Finder General.

TITLE PAGE IMAGE
Der Hexenmeister, seventeenth-century painting by
Domenicus van Wijnen. It contains many elements
popularly believed to be associated with witchcraft:
warlocks, wands, familiars and monstrous animals.

CONTENTS PAGE IMAGE
A Charge of Witchcraft by Henry Gillard Glindoni
(1852–1913).

ACKNOWLEDGEMENTS
I would like to thank my commissioning editor,
Ruth Sheppard, for her excellent work in tracking down
a truly vibrant set of illustrations and for her supremely
valuable guidance and advice throughout the process
of producing this book. I would also like to thank
Ariella Azoulay for her contributions to picture research.

IMAGE ACKNOWLEDGEMENTS
Images are reproduced courtesy of:

19th era/Alamy, page 3; blickwinkel/Alamy, page 43;
Bibliotheque des Arts Decoratifs, Paris, France/Archives
Charmet/The Bridgeman Art Library, page 28; eddie
linssen/Alamy, page 52 (top); Foto Ad Meskens, page 53;
Heritage Image Partnership Ltd/Alamy, page 38; Image
Asset Management Ltd/Alamy, pages 7, 22, 45 (bottom);
imagebroker/Alamy, page 14; INTERFOTO/Alamy, pages
20, 33 (bottom), 35 (top), 39; Lebrecht Music and Arts
Photo Library/Alamy, pages 26; Library of Congress, page
6, 41, 42, 44, 45 (top), 49, 50; Mar Photographics/Alamy,
page 54; Mary Evans Picture Library/Alamy, pages 4,
23, 24 (top), 30 (top), 32, 33 (top), 34, 48; Masterpics/
Alamy, page 12; North Wind Picture Archives/Alamy,
page 40; Peter Horree/Alamy, pages 10–11; PRISMA
ARCHIVO/Alamy, page 18; Private Collection/The
Stapleton Collection/The Bridgeman Art Library, page
21; Robert Benner, page 35; Shutterstock, page 13 (left);
Stuart Aylmer/Alamy, page 36; The Art Archive/Alamy,
page 30 (bottom); Tim1865, page 55; United Archives
GmbH/Alamy, page 52 (bottom).

THE WOODLAND TRUST
Shire Publications supports the Woodland Trust, the UK's
leading woodland conservation charity.

www.shirebooks.co.uk
To find out more about our authors and books visit our
website. Here you will find extracts, author interviews,
details of forthcoming events and the option to sign-up for
our newsletter.

CONTENTS

INTRODUCTION AND PRE-HISTORY

THE SUBJECT of witchcraft and witches endlessly intrigues every succeeding generation. As each age becomes more psychologically and technically sophisticated our interest in the reality and sometimes alien nature of witchcraft remains remarkably undiminished. It is tempting to view this interest as a hangover from the past and romanticism about a more primitive form of existence when mankind was somehow closer to nature.

As such, this apparently remote episode often fascinates because it involves beliefs and behaviour patterns that seem very obviously different to those of our modern and considered world. So why do we persist in wanting to study and understand what happened to these people (believers, witches and victims) and why? While it often seems a distant self-contained period of history that exerts a quirky hold over the imagination, strangely it is also familiar because some of its elements have important resonances with modern experience. The hunting and punishment of witches was very often a form of scapegoating – individuals blamed for the misfortunes of other individuals or of whole communities. We have our modern counterparts in the outbreaks of hatred towards bankers, foreigners and sex criminals and what they are believed to have done. We are also encouraged to understand such feelings through our creation of stereotypes of evil, ranging from Freddie Kruger to serial killers like Fred West or Ted Bundy. It could also be said that a taste for the supernatural has become considerably more in fashion since the 1990s than it had been for some time previously. The gothic 'dark' style is in vogue with heavy metal music witnessing something of a renaissance, while children's literature is full of references to magic, from the writings of Philip Pullman to the ultimately popular expression of this in J. K. Rowling's *Harry Potter* series.

Some social commentators also suggest Western society is experiencing a process of 're-enchantment' – a distrust of wholly rational explanations of the world and universe which has reawakened interest in more 'magical'

Opposite:
A Spanish witch flies to the sabbat on the back of a horned cloven-footed demon. Witchcraft in Spain was the subject of systematic war conducted by the Inquisition who, unlike their undeserved reputation, maintained sensible legal procedures, used torture very reluctantly and may have thus prevented witch-hunts in the area from getting out of hand the way they did further north.

'The Witch' by Albrecht Dürer, depicting a witch riding backwards on a goat, accompanied by four putti (winged male children), c. 1500.

outlooks. This leaves rational explanations of the world to become only one potential choice amongst many where they once claimed to rule. After all, the proportion of Americans who believe the lunar landing in 1969 was hoaxed in a warehouse rather than believe it really happened continues to grow. Evidence that our environment is turning against us – as it did during the period of the early modern witch-hunt – is all around. We are increasingly more attuned to environmental catastrophe and the marginal nature of existence in the Third World and areas that could flood as a result of global warming. Likewise, some economic and social prophets talk of the world being 'one bad harvest away from chaos' and the collapse of financial markets has re-introduced the First World spectacularly to a world of uncertainty, risk and irrationality. Just as numerous economic, social and cultural strains in the early modern period made people believe in irrational powers, so today, our faith in the benevolence of science is now weakened. There is distrust around issues in cloning, the fear of the consequence of genetically modified food – life again seems full of the 'drip, drip, drip' of risk, mundane and serious dangers.

Witches casting a spell to bring rain. Woodcut from Ulrich Molitor's *De Laniis et phitonicis mulieribus*, Constance, 1489.

However, the phenomenon of witchcraft is more correctly seen as an issue not so much of spells and past irrational modes of behaviour, but of the exercise of power. This particular factor can be seen everywhere in witchcraft's past and in its present. Theologians in the early modern period (*c.* 1400–1700) believed power had been dispensed to the Devil and those who sought to follow him. These same theologians also believed that they had a solemn duty to wield their own power to combat and destroy these people and thus preserve Christendom from its enemies. Some twentieth-century commentators were pressed into asking whether individuals themselves actually really believed they were in league with the Devil and were actually witches – or whether those persecuted for the crime of witchcraft were actually unfortunate victims of society's fears and spontaneous actions. Again the issue of power is evident since, while we cannot be certain what people believed, it is extremely likely that many who found themselves powerless within a rigid and inflexible society may have, in their mind, wanted to make such an agreement. In their own psyche and consciousness a pact with the Devil made them powerful and answered many of their concerns. The importance of power is also evident in the demise of witchcraft, as alternative explanations for events in the natural and human worlds became more sophisticated and powerful than witch beliefs.

In the early modern period witchcraft was prevalent in northern, southern and central Europe – France, Germany, Switzerland – extending north to Norway, Sweden and Finland, east to Russia and across the western seaboard to America and the Spanish territories of the new world. As such it was a universal phenomenon, common to all cultures. Witch-hunting in the early modern world was an episode more or less confined to a three-hundred-year period between 1450 and 1750. This was an age of considerable upheaval, during which the whole fabric of civilisation changed. Population levels fell as a result of constraints upon the physical environment. Agriculture became less productive, possibly caused by a sustained alteration in the physical climate as demonstrated in tree-ring data – which has led some historians to suggest that Europe experienced a 'mini ice age.' As a further result of these catastrophes the economies of Europe and America suffered a severe downturn. The dislocation caused by the squabbles of the Reformation and the religious wars that ensued augmented these troubles.

Beliefs about witches, magic and sorcery can be found in all the ancient cultures that spawned western European society. Witches appear in the Bible – Saul visited the witch of Endor – and there are also allusions to

Depiction of witches' sabbat, 1626.

A consultation with the witch, scene from a Latin comedy, depicted in a mosaic from the House of Cicero, Pompeii.

Following pages: *Saul and the Witch of Endor* (1526) by Jacob Cornelisz van Oostsanen, Dutch Netherlands. Having driven all magicians from Israel, King Saul disguised himself to consult the witch of Endor in order to contact the spirit of the prophet Samuel. Saul's suicide (in the middle background) on hearing the news he feared, is a warning against witchcraft.

magical practices. References also appeared in the Greek and Roman civilisations. Whilst frowned upon and considered inappropriate belief systems, they were not obviously identified with notions of evil. It is salutary in this respect that some early Roman commentators saw the early Christians in similar terms as later Christianity itself would see witches. Writing in the third century AD, Minucius Felix accused Christians of organising malevolent nocturnal meetings at which they practised unrestricted sexual activity and worshipped animals. He and others also believed that they indulged in cannibalism – a confused reference to the Christian Eucharist.

What was truly lacking from ancient beliefs about witches was an identification of witches with evil. This was also the case in early Christianity where there was little concern about the sources of evil in the universe.

Thirteenth-century
stained-glass
window from
Varennes-Jarcy
church (France),
depicting Theophilus
making a pact with
the Devil.

Although Satan had been named in the Bible, he was only personified
and given power over mankind in later writings. This process began from
the fifth century AD with the Christian assault on the gods of other cultures
who themselves became demonised. From destroying the temples and
shrines of these gods, it was a short step to incorporating their characteristics

into the Christian conception of evil. The Devil thus gradually came to acquire an identity. First the physical characteristics appeared, in the shape of cloven hooves and a goat's head. Secondly the desire to save believers from evil created an alternative system in which the Devil theoretically could have followers who – in doing his bidding – became enemies of the Christian world. These individuals were capable of making a dreadful contract with the Devil and thereby acquiring powers to use for evil and malevolent activity within the universe.

This concept was a product of the medieval world where attitudes to the idea of magic simultaneously began to change. Male magicians were tolerated and even celebrated at some European courts. There was also a strong element of what looks like magical belief in Christianity with individuals praying to saints for prosperity and sometimes for intervention, which was believed to manifest itself in miracles. Some wore amulets inscribed with biblical verses, consulted Christian mystics or wise men and women while others believed in the divine power held by images or the power of prophecy. Nonetheless religious authority was hostile to many magical practices and tried to stamp them out. In 1311 the Bishop of London ordered proceedings against magicians who claimed to find lost goods by means of sorcery. In English Church courts in the fifteenth century a number of individuals (both men and women) were prosecuted for using magical practices. The key to this was that the Christian churches were increasingly seeking to control what was considered legitimate magic and what was not. Increasingly this drew a distinction between what we might call types of conjuring trick, or harmless magic, and what came to be termed witchcraft.

The first papal pronouncement against witchcraft had been in 1258 when Pope Alexander IV condemned the practice. This effectively empowered papal inquisitions to examine individuals for the crimes of both

Rowan – this was believed to ward off the attacks of witches when placed outside the front entrance of a dwelling.

Horseshoe nailed to door. The eternal signifier of the desire to create 'good luck' in a society that believed in providence.

Kytelers Inn, in Kilkenny, Ireland, was established by Dame Alice Kyteler in the thirteenth century, and the sign of the inn still proclaims the association with witchcraft.

heresy and witchcraft. The early fourteenth century witnessed an isolated number of witchcraft trials with a political dimension, when members of the nobility were accused, or accused each other of the crime. The most famous of these in the British Isles was the case against Dame Alice Kyteler in Kilkenny, Ireland in 1324. Kyteler was accused of witchcraft by her late husband's family, who suspected she had caused his death by poison. Whilst she fled and escaped justice, her servant Petronella de Meath was burned at the stake. The trial demonstrated how a number of related accusations could paint a damaging picture of the accused. By 1400 much educated theological opinion was linking witchcraft with heresy so that contemporary thinking eventually made this opinion orthodox – meaning that to not believe in the heretical power of witches was itself becoming heresy.

On the eve of the prolific period of witch-hunting in Europe the archetype of the witch was in place and it is surprising how this stereotype has survived into the twenty-first century relatively unscathed. *The Wizard of Oz* and Disney versions of the witch embody many of the things early modern contemporaries were afraid of: an aged, ugly woman clothed in black, sitting by a cauldron with the attendant accessories of broomstick and herbs, and nurturing a relationship with her familiar (generally the black cat so despised by medieval Christendom). This lasting image explains elements of the history we have so far encountered – the witch is generally a woman and her long-term corruption by evil is emphasised through her ugly and aged appearance. Although the focus here suggests women were central to the archetype, places like Normandy notably hunted men in the sixteenth century and elsewhere the involvement of men and children in witchcraft is gradually coming to light. The witch is alone, devoid of other human company, emphasising at an early stage that she is a marginalised individual who only has contact with her familiar, and is most unlikely to have the protection and support of a family unit.

The black clothes (generally a cloak and hat covered with astral symbols) emphasise the link of witchcraft with earlier magical disciplines and practices. The appearance of the broomstick and the cauldron strongly emphasise the link between domesticity and the social world of squabbles, which led to accusations of witchcraft. Both items clearly had household uses, yet their sudden transformation into instruments of diabolical intent indicates how nervous society had become. The cooking pot could become the cauldron in which malevolent spells were hatched while the otherwise harmless broomstick became the means of transporting the witch to the sabbat where, with her compatriots, she would worship the devil and do his bidding. These images haunted the psychological map of Europe for three hundred years and the enduring interest in these phenomena is ample evidence that all societies want to know why.

Flight of the witches, miniature in a manuscript by Martin Le France, 1450.

WITCHCRAFT AND WITCH-HUNTING TAKE HOLD

Although there were a number of isolated high-profile cases in the fourteenth century, the obsession with witches and the overwhelming need to stamp out witchcraft really took hold of European society in the fifteenth century. Up to this point, more or less in keeping with the image of witches in many folk fairy tales, these individuals were suspected of merely doing harm to others – this was, however, to change. As the fifteenth century dawned, accusations of witchcraft increasingly contained the notion of a pact with the Devil. This made those accused seem to increasingly resemble what the historian Christina Larner, writing about Scottish witch-hunts, termed 'Enemies of God' rather than being simply associated with species of magic. The upsurge in interest at the start of the fifteenth century fed, and was fed by, the appearance of various demonological works of literature. This link was an important factor in explaining the prevalence of witch trials and also partly explains the decline in witchcraft trials and witch-hunting in the early part of the sixteenth century – when several important works that informed Christian Europe about witches, and what they could do, fell out of print. Likewise many intellectuals were caught up in writing and arguing about the nature of the religious reformation that was sweeping through Europe. This link has persuaded some to see the witch-hunt as promoted by the gentry and intellectuals of Europe. Certainly it is possible to argue that where they expressed concern and interest in the phenomenon of witchcraft, accusations against individuals were more likely to be taken seriously and be pursued. In areas where the gentry and rulers were disinterested in the idea, witch-hunts were far less likely to occur.

A legal revolution in Europe made witch-hunts more likely since it brought a greater emphasis upon the punishment of offences and because it created a number of decentralised legal systems, whereby inquisitors and legal personnel could inquire in localities about suspected witches. This enabled individuals to offer evidence against their neighbours with relatively little risk, making prolonged witch-hunts more likely. This also encouraged

Opposite:
Execution scene from the chronicle of Schilling of Lucerne, illustrating the burning of a woman in Willisau, Switzerland, in 1447.

smaller states and city jurisdictions to take power for themselves and hunt out local witches. It was especially noted in the fifteenth century that the detection and prosecution of witches was enthusiastically taken up by the lay magistracy, when it had previously been the preserve of ecclesiastical

authority. This legal system – referred to as the 'inquisitorial system' – was prevalent in Europe but was not a feature of the English legal system, which has been described as 'accusatorial'. This name rightly suggests that the legal system in England placed much more responsibility upon the accuser, who had to back up his or her accusation in court and face both the person they had accused and the opinion of their whole community. This much more daunting prospect, it has been suggested, led to considerably fewer prosecutions of individuals for witchcraft in England.

Legal and religious texts added to an increasingly sophisticated body of knowledge outlining the nature of the Devil and how he could perform a number of actions that demonstrated his supernatural powers. He could change his form and in particular assume the appearance of a man. Likewise, many didactic stories well into the eighteenth century have him in the guise of a handsome man using his powers of persuasion upon unsuspecting and 'weak' women.

By the end of the fourteenth century theological works had come to rely upon the Ten Commandments as the basis of Christian doctrine. This transformed how people viewed the earlier, apparently innocent forms of magical practice. This theology became linked with the idea that the pact individuals made with the Devil placed obligations upon them to worship him. Such a pact enabled them to allegedly alter the weather, cure diseases or transport themselves to far-distant places (generally using the power of flight – itself supremely unnatural). Nonetheless, for all these privileges these individuals were duty-bound to give homage to the Devil. Thus the idea of the witches' sabbat (or meeting) was born – an idea that was to have an enduring and arguably catastrophic hold upon the early modern European imagination. The use of the word 'imagination' here is deliberate since depictions of it were a collection of fears and inversions of civilised practices. Thus, in the imagination, religious relics and symbols were defiled, sexual norms were inverted and human flesh was consumed – in the 1430s Johannes Nideran announced he had been told that witches devoured their own children. These transgressions were compounded by the active worship of the Devil in obscene ways that mocked the worship of God and Jesus. The construction of these inversions, in a range of literature of the period, does lend credibility to the theories of some historians who have suggested early modern Europeans began to live in an increasingly psychologically dangerous and overwhelmingly oppressive environment.

One of the most influential works – which gives us a flavour of this environment – was the *Malleus Maleficarum* ('Hammer of Witches'), which began to exert a presence in witchcraft circles from its appearance in 1487. This was precisely because, as an authoritative text, it was portable enough to convey these new learned ideas across Europe. Long thought compiled

Opposite: Witches' sabbat in a nineteenth-century painting by Spanish painter Goya. Compare this later depiction with that on page 8.

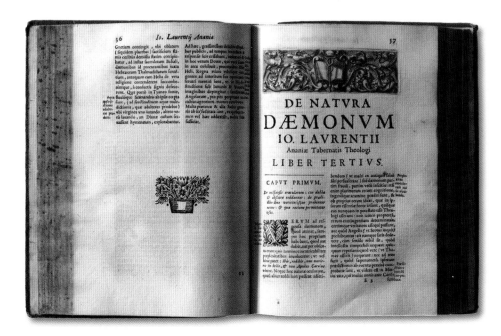

Malleus Maleficarum (The 'Hammer of Witches'), 2nd tome, Lyon 1669. First published in 1486 in Speyer, the Hexenhammer is a guide to witch-hunting. It describes how to recognise witches and shows methods for interrogation, torture and punishment. The book has been held responsible for triggering some of the worst excesses of witch trials.

by two Dominican inquisitors, Heinrich Kramer and Jacob Sprenger, its precise authorship has become disputed in more recent years, partly because its contents seem particularly far-fetched and hysterical. What is scarcely in doubt is the all-pervading influence of this work, which has been described as one of the most misogynist works ever written. It was influential because it claimed both a considerable breadth and depth of authority. The *Malleus* portrayed women as especially susceptible to evil and the machinations of the Devil because of various aspects of their altogether-different nature to men. The writers of the *Malleus* saw women as having a reputation for wickedness inherited from biblical texts. This was compounded by a belief that they were spiteful (often to other women), impressionable and thus more likely to be impressed by the flattery of the Devil. They were also strong-willed and would lead themselves into trouble but, above all, the authors considered women to be sexually rapacious. Thus this reputation would seal their fate as slaves to diabolical will and power, often into old age. All this would supposedly provoke them to commit sexual acts with the Devil, indulge in acts of cannibalism with the bodies of new-born children and, as midwives, actively kill children in the womb or offer the new-born children to the Devil himself. This work and its influence has perhaps done too much to fix in our minds the idea of women as witches and this has, for some centuries, obscured the involvement of men and children as protagonists and victims caught up in witch-hunts.

In the fifteenth century the first recognisable full-scale witch-hunts began to appear in parts of Europe. Some historians note that probably the first of these occurred in western Switzerland in the 1430s, roughly at the time that an important theological council took place in Basel, attended by churchmen and intellectuals. This conference of opinions was alarmed to hear reports of witches in the locality and evidence from their prosecution quickly made them appear part of a deliberate and malevolent conspiracy against Christianity. These built upon some other ideas that had developed in learned circles elsewhere in Switzerland. This development in this part of Europe was interesting since this geographical area was a meeting point for ideas from all parts of the European Christian mainland. The lead in investigating them was also taken by states in the region that were ambitious to establish their own independence. From these beginnings, witch trials spread slowly to other cities in Europe, appearing in quite virulent form in France with some isolated outbreaks in parts of Italy. Eventually this spread to the Holy Roman Empire, appearing in German cities including Heidelberg, Cologne and Metz.

By the middle of the sixteenth century the fear of witches and the beliefs surrounding their diabolical activities had escalated to the extent that the active desire of these evil people to break the laws of nature was central to the threat they posed. This is one reason that accusations of homosexual activity started to enter the canon of witchcraft ideas. The importance of these ideas, and their rapid spread throughout Europe, were of long-lasting

The Devil baptising a male witch in a corruption of Christian church rituals. From Friar M. Guaccius' *Compendium Maleficarum, c.* 1608.

Witch raising a storm to wreck a ship and drown sailors. Witches would also often be suspected of raising storms to destroy crops. Woodcut from *Historia de gentibus septentrionalibus*, Antwerp, 1562, by Olaus Magnus.

influence upon the history of witchcraft and their significance is difficult to overstate. This represents an episode in history where knowledge, inspired and driven by fear, was transferred from intellectual circles to the populace at large. The recurrence of such cycles in more recent times inspired the American playwright Arthur Miller to write his dramatic masterpiece *The Crucible* – to liken early modern witch-hunting at Salem, Massachusetts to the search for communist agitators in 1950s McCarthyite America.

Certainly the spread of ideas from intellectuals to the populace at large very dramatically shaped how witchcraft accusations, and the hunt for witches, would play out in certain countries and localities. In England, for example, there was very little if any discussion of the idea of the witch's sabbat so that crime was generally conceived of solely as committing types of harmful magic (termed *maleficium*). In part this served to explain why witchcraft and witch-hunting was a more marginal activity in England than in parts of central Europe. Scotland, in particular, provides very good evidence for the idea that witchcraft could be spread by the application of intellectual ideas to real-life experiences. In 1590 James VI of Scotland (later James I of England) became intensely interested in continental witchcraft ideas while he was in Denmark. When he brought his wife (Anne of Denmark) back to Scotland terrible storms placed all on board his ship at grave risk, which led James to believe he was the victim of a conspiracy of witches, later discovered to reside around the town of North Berwick.

James himself was progressively drawn in to the investigation, and eventual interrogation of one witch in particular, Agnes Sampson, who was later executed. James's fascination with witchcraft continued and, in 1597, he wrote his own treatise on witchcraft entitled *Daemonologie*, which further promoted the idea of witch-hunting. Some have also seen the writing and performance of Shakespeare's *Macbeth* (c. 1606) as linked to James's interests. Likewise the play also provided another method for witchcraft, and beliefs about it, to enter the public domain and be consumed.

Thus, by the end of the sixteenth century there was a whole body of beliefs in witches, witchcraft, and the powers that both of these possessed in place. Christian society, whether Catholic or Protestant, had come to believe in the reality of witchcraft. In the central parts of Europe individuals, rulers, theologians and those who administered justice genuinely believed that there existed a conspiracy against their Christian community. This conspiracy gave evil people powers that they used against the innocent; they also worshipped ungodly idols and indulged in ungodly practices. As such they were a threat that could not be tolerated, for the safety of Christian society as a whole. The power of these beliefs bequeathed authority to various forms of justice throughout Europe to take action. Some of this was probably unofficial action where mobs and crowds took justice into

North Berwick witches flying widdershins around a church, some on broomsticks. Widdershins means counter-clockwise or more pertinently left-handed, associated with inversion and the Devil.

An engraving of James VI of Scotland examining the North Berwick witches, from the pamphlet *Newes from Scotland* (1591). James wrote the treatise *Daemonologie* condemning witchcraft six years later. Agnes Sampson, Agnes Tompson and others were tried before King James: most were executed.

their own hands – it will probably never be known how many unfortunate individuals perished in this manner. Elsewhere individuals were arrested and processed through official systems of justice. This could result in imprisonment, in fines, or in banishment from the community. In many instances, however, it also attracted the ultimate penalty of execution. In many parts of Europe this followed the biblical punishment of burning at the stake. However in other places, including England, witches were hanged as a species of common criminal. It is also worth remembering that the systems of justice also enabled some to be acquitted, where evidence against them was insubstantial, or hearsay and merely circumstantial.

Thus, over a period of two hundred and fifty years, Christian society in Western Europe built up a series of beliefs which were intended to protect it from a dangerous and diabolical enemy. By 1600 these beliefs had reached their widest scope and ambition and it would take considerable changes in the ideological landscape before their logic was comprehensively questioned.

The witches in William Shakespeare's *Macbeth*, painted by John Downman (c. 1824).

Opposite:
The Hexenturm (Witches' Tower) in Hofheim am Taunus, near Frankfurt, Germany, where women accused of witchcraft were imprisoned, or awaited their trials. Visible on the wall is the plaque to the women burnt nearby as witches.

THE HIGH POINT AND HEYDAY OF WITCHES AND WITCH-HUNTING

WITCH-HUNTING was probably at its height during the second half of the sixteenth century and the first half of the seventeenth century. If we look at a map of Europe during this period we can see an interesting comparison between how witchcraft was perceived and dealt with in a number of European countries. Countries on the edge of Europe – such as England, Scotland, Spain and Portugal in the west; Norway, Sweden, Finland in the north; Greece, Poland and Russia in the east – all witnessed periodic witch-hunts but these resulted in a comparatively low level of executions for witchcraft. Norway and Finland, for example executed roughly 38 per cent and 16 per cent respectively of those prosecuted. This has generally led historians to conclude that prosecution with lesser punishment indicates that the crime of witchcraft was considered less serious in such localities and it would periodically die out altogether. However in the centre of Europe it really was a different story. France, Luxembourg, Switzerland and parts of the Low Countries witnessed some very significant witch-hunts with much higher levels of execution – Luxembourg executed 69 per cent of convicted witches between 1509 and 1687. However even these were dwarfed by the level of witch-hunting which occurred in Germany. The German lands (comprising the whole of modern Germany and what is now Austria) were to become the very cradle of the European witch-hunt, eventually coming to account for more than the rest of the early modern world's total of witchcraft prosecutions and executions put together. At this time Germany was effectively a patchwork quilt of small states, principalities and independent cities, all with their own identity and often their own system of local jurisdiction, both of which they embraced and protected. When the associated issues of religious upheaval caused by the Reformation are taken into account both these factors helped to create the perfect conditions for witch-hunting to flourish.

Although Germany was split into these numerous states, they were – in theory – all governed, to a lesser or greater extent, by the Carolina legal

Opposite:
A witches' coven brewing potions, sixteenth-century woodcut, by Hans Baldung Grien.

An illustration in a pamphlet showing three witches being burned alive at the stake in Derneburg in 1555. This was a common method of execution in Europe.

Ein erschröckliche geschicht/ so zu Derneburg in der Graff-schafft Reinstepn/am Hartz gelegen/von dreyen Zauberin/vnd zwayen Mañen/Jn etlichen tagen des Monats Octobris Jm 1 5 5 5. Jare ergangen ist.

Opposite:
One of a series of woodblocks made by the German artist Albrecht Dürer in the late fifteenth century, at the height of witch-hunting. The woman or whore of Babylon rides a seven-headed dragon, leaving a trail of destruction behind her, including (on the right) a riverside city in flames.

code of 1532. This made it a clear and obvious offence to associate with witches, witchcraft or related phenomena. If an individual was named as having been involved with these things then they could be convicted and punished by burning at the stake – the penalty prescribed by the Carolina code. Some of these provisions, whether wittingly or unwittingly, were tailor-made to ensure that the hunt for witches and their prosecution would gather momentum and feed off previous prosecutions. One further fact that influenced this momentum was the sporadic use of torture to extract confessions. Torture was justified by judges who argued that witchcraft was a *crimen exceptum* (exceptional crime) justifying extreme measures. These issues were important and did not differ significantly between Catholic and Protestant states or rulers. Once torture and its use became widespread there was an active dynamic that ensured those tortured implicated others in a cycle that could rapidly repeat itself many times in the same locality. This occurred in places like Rottenburg in 1585, Ellwangen in 1611, Offenburg in 1627–30 and, as we shall see, Bamberg in 1630.

Witch trials in Germany accelerated after the 1570s and probably the biggest single instance was the spate of trials that occurred in Trier

between 1587 and 1593 where at least 368 people – and possibly more – were executed at the stake. The speed and the intensity of such witch-hunts could snare all sorts of people for all sorts of reasons. The Trier witch-hunt even resulted in the rector of the University, Dietrich Flade, being accused of witchcraft and suffering the ultimate punishment. Suspicion had fallen upon him because, in his professional capacity as a legal officer, he had doubted the value and use of torture. The pattern established in Trier was replicated at other times in other German cities. Würzburg witnessed a mini outbreak in 1616, whilst a more significant and far-reaching hunt began in 1626 and lasted for five years. By the time the hunt petered out it had claimed the lives of between 200 and 250 of the city's citizens, with many hundreds from the surrounding areas also prosecuted and executed.

Another significant series of trials occurred in Bamberg, happening contemporaneously with those at Würzburg at the end of the 1620s.

We know a lot about some aspects of this hunt because some important and interesting documents survive. Looking closely at this particular witch-hunt can tell us a great deal about the motives and behaviour of those caught up in this historical episode. It also displays many of the typical characteristics that we have encountered already. Bamberg was so disconcerted and uneasy about the issue of witchcraft

The public hanging of three Chelmsford witches, Joan Prentice, Joan Cony and Joan Upney, an illustration from an English pamphlet of 1589.
Before them roam their named familiars, such names probably emerged during confessions.

that it produced a document – a prosecution manual to help those trying to trap culprits. This contained 101 questions to ask at a witchcraft trial and these involved forcefully persuading all those present to acknowledge the deep reality of witchcraft, and likewise the existence of witches as a concrete and terrible threat to the community. If individuals denied accusations against them then torture was resorted to, with a grim record of success.

One individual prosecuted during this terror was the town's Burgomaster, an individual named Johannes Junius, and documents about his trial survive which provide the very human dimension to what was otherwise a cruel and clinical legal procedure. The court's deposition against Junius, dated Wednesday 18 June 1628, states that Junius categorically denied being a witch and attending the witches' sabbat. This denial was then countered by the testimony of a doctor and a servant who both claimed they had seen him at two separate witch gatherings.

Opposite: Women accused of witchcraft were often subjected to torture, as it was believed that they would feel no pain if they were indeed witches protected by the Devil.

Bamberg's witch-house, etching from 1627.

A Swiss woman accused of witchcraft is burnt at the stake.

Junius, so the transcript says, continued to deny his guilt despite persuasion from the authorities who had imprisoned him. His denials led to the use of thumbscrews and then leg screws to extract a confession, although Junius bravely continued with his protestations of innocence. It can clearly be seen how denial, in this instance, was greeted with an escalation in torture – after the leg screws Junius was exposed to the strappado, where he was suspended by the arms in a rope device, then dropped from a considerable height. This method, which would have caused immense pain, was used even though Junius was at this time in late middle age.

Although this torture also provoked denials, Junius appeared at a subsequent hearing ready and prepared to confess his guilt. His story of involvement in witchcraft also tells us much about how the court and individuals thought witchcraft worked and ought to work because, whether true or not, the confession seemed plausible and accepted. Junius admitted that he had lost an expensive lawsuit in 1624 and had brooded upon this misfortune in a local orchard. Whilst there a young countrywoman had appeared to him and asked him why he was so deep in thought and apparently so sorry for himself. Once the conversation began the woman persuaded Junius to submit to her will and when this had been achieved transformed instantly into a goat – the time-honoured symbol of the Devil – declaring 'Now you see with whom you have had to do. You must be mine or I will forthwith break your neck.' Although Junius, according to this testimony, tried to resist this, the Devil came back with a great multitude of his disciples, all of them intent on pressurising Junius to renounce God and the saints. Thereafter the woman who had appeared to him agreed to be his lover and to shower him with gifts of money and other powers. According to this testimony Junius had been given the use of a diabolical black dog to convey him to the witches' sabbat. Junius's diabolical lover had also incited Junius to kill both his own son and daughter. The Devil also met Junius and told him that although he would be arrested for witchcraft, the Devil would enable him to prevail against his accusers and interrogators. This particular confession demonstrates how the authorities were scared of the man they had captured and imprisoned. Unfortunately a confession of this nature was enough to ensure the guilt of Junius, and he was subsequently executed.

Junius — outraged and bitter about the accusations made against him — secretly wrote and smuggled out a letter intended for the eyes of his grieving daughter. The letter survived and gives a unique insight into the reality behind Junius's experience. The contents of the

Witches bewitch a victim while she sleeps.

letter bring home the paranoia of those charged with hunting down and bringing witches to justice, and also some of the very down-to-earth and human responses of those involved. In his letter Junius utterly denies being a witch or associating with witches. However those questioning him don't believe him, particularly since they have been told that witches have the power to resist interrogation. Therefore Junius discovers that his captors will either make him confess voluntarily, or force one out of him through torture. When he refused to confess, the torturer uses the thumbscrews on him and then the strappado no fewer than eight times. Ironically, rather than the Devil providing Junius with the power to withstand torture, he tells his daughter that his trust in God's mercy and strength was all that protected him. Thus far Junius had resisted but the torturer took him aside and, obviously preoccupied with guilt and compassion, persuaded him to confess anything he could think of to make the torture stop. A good Christian, Junius was still not convinced since he believed he would be committing a sin by lying! After some thought Junius decided his only way out was to confess a range of imaginary offences and then seek absolution from a priest for telling such lies. After Junius had confessed, the officials asked him to name those he had seen at his diabolical revels. When he said he had recognised nobody they threatened him again with the torturer's tools. His letter then records with regret that he was made, in his mind, to walk down the streets of the town accusing people who lived at specific houses – despite the fact that, as his letter says, he actually knew none of

This early sixteenth-century woodcut depicts a witch having intercourse with the Devil.

In a seventeenth-century Dutch court, a woman is weighed to prove whether she is a witch.

these people personally. Junius was then asked about his own crimes and had to be threatened further when he refused to talk about them. This dreadful tale ends with Junius noting that each of those who had accused him had sought his forgiveness for lying about his involvement in witchcraft when they went to their execution. Last of all Junius asked his daughter to keep the letter secret, so that the jailer who had helped him by smuggling it out would not be executed for this kindly action.

The story of Junius gives an unparalleled insight into how witch-hunting could spread and escalate at such an alarming rate and demonstrates how some of the beliefs and procedures dramatically fed this escalation.

Those arrested for witchcraft, like Junius, had been implicated by others forced to 'confess' earlier in the cycle. From this point onwards it was considered their duty to confess, either voluntarily or if necessary through torture – which could be used progressively because witches were alleged to be able to resist such things. This made a further confession almost certain and the fortitude Junius showed in the face of such cruelty is something of an exception. Moreover when Junius finally did confess it was not enough to admit he was a witch. He had to confess his crimes – which he had to make up and make plausible to those interrogating him. Even this was not enough: victims like Junius had to also implicate others who would be arrested, beginning the entire cycle again.

Friedrich Spee (1591–1635), German Jesuit, poet, and opponent of trials for witchcraft.

This story also shows us some of the all-too-human reactions to this situation. Faced by overwhelming odds Junius was brave and noble, relying upon the goodness and mercy of his God. The torturers and jailers were moved to compassion and the previous victims who had implicated Junius asked his forgiveness for what they had been led into saying. It is also possible to see the determination and callousness of Junius's captors, determined to make him confess by using various pressures – some sanctioned by law, some arguably beyond it. Finally, the sheer level of fear and responsibility felt by these people should not be forgotten, caught up in the midst of a witch panic and a witch-hunt over which they arguably had no control – it was precisely these dynamics and mechanisms of witch-hunting that produced the events at Bamberg at the end of the 1620s. The virulent 1631 hunt in the city of Würzburg persuaded a Jesuit, Friedrich Spee, to write a fierce condemnation of the judicial system that produced convictions on flimsy evidence and under intense duress. This scepticism would also be evident elsewhere. In

Woodcut depicting two executions at the stake.

Sweden in the 1670s, for example, lawyers began to have markedly less confidence in the evidence they were presenting and the number of prosecutions entered a clear decline in this country.

Thus we have seen that, in its heyday, witch-hunting could ravage whole communities and it was only during the following century that the practice began to decline as interest in witchcraft and witch-hunting diminished.

THE DECLINING YEARS
OF WITCH-HUNTING

THE SEVENTEENTH CENTURY saw the regularity and intensity of witch-hunting start to decline, before it disappeared more or less completely by the middle of the eighteenth century. Nonetheless this period did witness some notable episodes, which have often been considered by historians to be valuable for developing theories as to how and why witch-hunting happened.

As noted, England was scarcely a vibrant centre of witch-hunting, partly caused by its system of justice, which undermined the on-going dynamics and 'domino effect' that led to hunts like the one in Bamberg. Likewise, there was an incomplete conception of witchcraft and witch beliefs in England, especially when compared to European societies. Some historians have noted how the more favourable economic position of women in English society may well have protected them from some of the worst aspects of behaviour aimed at controlling them and their destiny. Compared to many societies in continental Europe, women in England were far more likely to have some degree of independence, status and respect and were also more likely to own property.

Nonetheless in the mid-seventeenth century there was an episode that had a specific impact upon the history of witch-hunting in England. In the years just before the middle of the century there was one particular witch-hunt in East Anglia that effectively made the county of Essex the epicentre of witch-hunting in England (there were similar contemporary episodes in Spain and France). During the years of the English Civil War the broad area of East Anglia witnessed the activities of the self-styled Witch Finder General, a religious fanatic called Matthew Hopkins. In some respects a shadowy figure, Hopkins commenced his pursuit of witches towards the end of 1644, and his activities only ceased with his retirement and early death in 1647. Between these dates Hopkins toured eastern England in search of evidence that witches were at work in local communities. In many of these communities Hopkins and his assistant John Sterne were actively

Opposite:
A witch's ducking stool displayed at the Old Gaol House in King's Lynn, Norfolk.

welcomed and they received a reasonable income from this work, often raised by local municipal authorities. Hopkins and Sterne operated largely outside of the law and claimed to be agents of a special commission to find and prosecute witches. They generally employed less direct methods of persuasion on suspects than those used in Bamberg. Sleep deprivation – which many modern psychologists argue is arguably more effective than more direct physical forms of torture – was a particularly popular technique. They also searched victims for signs of the witch's mark: protrusions, warts and irregularities that could conceivably be methods of suckling familiars. The discovery of such irregularities – scarcely difficult to find in a population of significant enough size – further served to enhance and promote the activities of Hopkins and Sterne.

The Witch Gown of Veringenstadt, 1680. Found in the collection of the Historisches Museum der Pfalz Speyer, it was probably worn when individuals were examined and questioned.

Not surprisingly individuals confessed to conversing with the Devil in the shape of a number of animals, and even having sex with him. Alongside such crimes individuals also pleaded guilty to taking malevolent action against their neighbours and harbouring imps and familiars to do their bidding. 'Mother Clarke' of Lawford was tried at Chelmsford in 1645 and was partly damned by the confession of Rebecca West, who confessed that her mother had taken her to a meeting of witches and pressed upon her the importance of never repeating what she was to witness. Rebecca West said that she saw the Devil appear to her as a black dog which then kissed her three times. At a later date the Devil appeared in the guise of a handsome young man who took her as his bride and the couple had sex. Later in proceedings a religious minister from just outside Colchester testified that he believed his horse had been bewitched by 'Mother Clarke', who persuaded it to throw him with the intention of breaking his neck. In all Hopkins and Sterne were arguably responsible for the deaths of a hundred people (almost all of them women) and irreparably damaging the lives of a significantly greater number.

This episode has persuaded some historians to note that witch-hunting could be promoted by an individual who was willing to make it an obsession, or career, to root out witches and bring them to justice. Interestingly this episode also introduced some elements of belief from the Continent (the figure of the Devil loomed larger here than in previous English hunts) and this emphasis may also have come from Hopkins himself. Certainly there is plenty of evidence that witch-hunting persisted where there were individuals who had an active interest in its continuation.

The Essex witch-hunts have also persuaded some other historians to consider whether there was a pattern to who was likely to be accused of the crime. The noted historian Alan McFarlane discovered that accusers were of a higher social status than those who tended to be accused. He saw this as a symptom of underlying social tension where those who were becoming prosperous grew to dislike the dependence and marginality of those with significantly less secure economic status. This became a major interpretation of witchcraft and its significance in England. However what was equally significant about this episode is that it occurred where the administration of justice was weak. The justice system in England was in turmoil as a result of the civil war, but equally Hopkins and Sterne actively created their own mandate for their actions, which ran way beyond the intentions of conventional justice. This was in stark contrast to the events at Bamberg where mainstream justice was central to the action.

Arguably the last major event of witch-hunting in the English-speaking world, and one of the last in the wider European world, was the outburst in colonial America at the end of the seventeenth century, which occurred at Salem, Massachusetts. In January 1692 a number of young girls began to exhibit fits and other forms of outrageous behaviour. A doctor attending them immediately diagnosed that they were victims of forms of witchcraft and the community began searching for the witches involved. In the panic that followed, many established legal procedures were ditched in favour of more immediate, but significantly less sound, forms of justice. In particular the court at Salem began to accept what became

A German four-edged thrusting blade, a so-called 'Hexenstecher', with a hexagram inscribed on the handle, and the date '1691'. It was widely assumed that the devil had placed a mark on the bodies of his followers, a mark insensitive to pain and which would not bleed if pierced. In the course of a witch trial, a prosecutor would try to find this mark – often thought to be a dubiously shaped birthmark or wart. Once discovered it would be stabbed with a knife; if the suspect showed no reaction, he or she was further suspected of involvement in witchcraft.

known as 'spectral' evidence – namely the assertion by an accuser that they had been the victim of a witch appearing to them as a spirit or a ghost. Quite obviously – to us – such forms of evidence were manifestly open to considerable abuse and malice on the part of accusers, but this simple factor did not seem relevant or appropriate to an intensely frightened community. By the time the hunt had burnt itself out, twenty individuals had been executed and as many as seventeen had died in prison.

The witch-hunt at Salem is especially valuable to historians because there survives probably the greatest and most detailed evidence of any early modern witch-hunt. This is largely because it occurred comparatively late in the cycle of witch-hunts, when record keeping and the machinery of law and government had become more sophisticated and precise. Likewise,

Seventeenth-century New England colonists arresting a woman suspected of witchcraft.

Salem was a comparatively new 'transplanted' community with an intensely Puritan ethic, which meant that the whole phenomenon of witches and witchcraft was taken especially seriously. Investigating what happened at Salem has also encouraged subsequent generations of historians to link together a wide range of very different historical sources to build up a picture of the community. For example, by looking at land records investigators were able to suggest that some accusations may have been the continuation of a generations-old squabble over land – evident when accusers and accused came from the two sides of the quarrel. Others were able to examine the strained relations between this community and its religious minister, Samuel Parris, who the community had tried to get rid of the previous year. The survival of many other records point to other factors that may have been important in giving the witch-hunt the flavour of a local community squabble. Historians have seen that two families (the Porters and the Putnams) were struggling for the leading position in the community. To those looking closely it seems no coincidence that those associated with

Late nineteenth-century illustration of the Salem witch-hunt. Suspected witches are put in the stocks while locals look on.

these two respective families would frequently find themselves on different sides of witchcraft accusations. Likewise the rural community of Salem Village was in conflict with the increasingly economically prosperous areas of Salem associated with trade and commerce, further stoking elements of social tension.

The Salem episode also brings to light another possible explanation for why witches were feared and hunted. Some historians believe that outbreaks of witch-hunting have psychological explanations rooted in the attention-seeking behaviour of adolescent girls. However recently there has been offered another physiological explanation, as there is evidence from a number of localities that suggests individuals may have been suffering from Ergot poisoning. Ergot is a fungus that grows upon the cereal crop rye, a widely grown food staple in early modern Europe and North America. This fungus has a molecular structure very similar to lysergic acid (LSD), which

The trial of George Jacobs of Salem for witchcraft. Nineteenth-century illustration by Tompkins Harrison Matteson.

is capable of producing both hallucinations and violent, uncontrollable muscle spasms and convulsions. This fungus grows on rye when it is particularly damp and wet and – where diary or other evidence permits – it has been possible to link evidence of witch-hunting and witchcraft incidents to evidence of such poor weather conditions. Likewise the proximity and consumption of rye, in various forms, can be linked to these incidents. Whilst it would be far-fetched to suggest this was a central cause, it may explain some incidents. Evidence from one outbreak of witch-hunting in northern Norway produced vital archive material which described individual's symptoms after they had consumed bread or beer made from rye – in some instances inventory and diary evidence recorded what these people consumed before their hallucinatory episode. Some of these individuals suffered the delusion they were under attack but, significantly, some suffered from the delusion that they themselves were in fact witches and could cast spells and perform superhuman acts. These same links between the cultivation of rye and poor weather have been offered as explanations for the episode at Salem with some justification. Rye was grown there in low-lying marshy areas, whilst contemporary diaries record especially poor weather in the lead-up to the outbreak of witchcraft allegations. The leading advocate for this theory, toxicologist Linda Caporael, was convinced she had found the clinching evidence in a diary entry which claims to show that a dog had gone into convulsions immediately after eating a 'witch cake' made from rye flour.

The fungus Ergot, which grows on rye: Ergot poisoning has been suggested as a possible explanation for the Salem witch-hunt among others.

Unlike many other explanations, historians have been able to test and view the effects of Ergot poisoning both in the laboratory and in real-world incidents. Most powerfully and tragically an outbreak of such poisoning in a post-war French town provided evidence of individuals hallucinating and suffering terrifying convulsions – the latter memorably caught on film. Unfortunately several inhabitants died before the authorities tracked down the source of the Ergot, which had found its way into a batch of flour used by the local bakery.

Just as with the Essex witch-hunts conducted by Matthew Hopkins and John Sterne, this seventeenth-century episode really demonstrated that witchcraft accusations could still occur where

SOME LEGENDS
OF THE NEW ENGLAND COAST.

By Mrs. Harriet Prescott Spofford.

ILLUSTRATED.

III.

SALEM.—(CONCLUDED.)

It is a common error to suppose that the three learned professions lead the people in point of intelligence. On the contrary, trained in grooves not easy to leave, they remain as they were in the beginning, and almost all advance comes from the outside. This was never better exemplified than in the Witchcraft delusion. If the physicians then had possessed either acuteness, skill, or candor, they would have checked the girls in their first spasms; if the ministers had been what they should have been ere daring to undertake the cure of souls, instead of lending countenance to their pretensions and praying over the girls, they would have punished them and made them fear the consequences of their manœuvres; if the lawyers had exercised any quality which a lawyer should possess, they would have sifted the testimony till it blew away in the wind, and would have utterly cast out the evidence of spectres, instead of greedily receiving it and hounding on the poor wretches to their death. When justices, deacons, doctors and gentry hurried to wonder over and sympathize with the young impostors, when their leaders came to be mad, it is no marvel that the people lost their head and followed after. In the faith that the girls were bewitched, and that Satan acted only through human agencies, they clamored to know who it was that had bewitched them; and thus beset, the girls, either at random or because there was no one to befriend her, or at Mr. Parris's half-hinted suggestion, timidly pronounced a name. "Good," they said, "Good"—cheating their consciences, perhaps, by making it only a surname; they had no such timidity by-and-by; and Sarah Good was consequently apprehended. When she was examined, two others had been named, arrested, and were examined with her.

Sarah Good was a poor creature—homeless, destitute, deserted by her husband, with a family of children to support by odds and ends of work, by begging from door to door, and scraping together in any way what little she could. Doubtless she was a nuisance in the neighborhood, as most impecunious and shiftless people are, and her reputation was not satisfactory. Her fate was certain from the onset. The people—who were full of horror

PRUSSIA.—THE LANDWEHRMAN'S CHRISTMAS FURLOUGH.—SEE PAGE 347.

and of pity for the tortured girls; who had been told by the physicians that they were bewitched; who had seen the ministers oracularly confirm this statement; who had heard Mr. Parris make it the subject of his vehement discourses Sunday after Sunday, while the distemper of the girls alarmed the congregation; who had lately done nothing but look for the guilty author of this diabolism, drew a breath of relief when at last the witch was named; so plausible a person, a vagrant and friendless; and it must be admitted that Sarah Good and Mrs. Osburne—an elderly person, sometimes bedridden, sometimes distracted, who absented herself from meeting—and the slave Tituba, were the best possible selections that the cunning hussies could have made; and the people were satisfied. Mrs. Osburne died in prison nine months afterward; Tituba confessed—as she subsequently averred, under stress of beatings from Mr. Parris—and, lying in jail a year and a month, was finally sold for her fees; but Sarah Good drank her cup, bitter all her life long, to the bitter dregs. The meeting-house was thronged at her examination; she was placed on a platform in full sight of all there; Mr. Parris had excited every one with his impassioned opening prayer; the array of magistrates, marshal and constable more enough to strike awe into her soul at any time, much more when her life was at stake. Acquainted with want, with sorrow and obloquy, her heart had been hardened, and she gave back no mild answers to the catechising. The justices assumed her guilt to be already established, endeavored to make her involve herself, gave leading questions to the witnesses, allowed all manner of abominable interruptions, and browbeat and abused her. When the afflicted children were introduced, as a glance of her eye they straightway fainted and went into spasms, cried out that they were pinched and pricked and throttled, and fell stiff as the dead. Upon being taken to her and touched by her, the color returned to their faces, their limbs relaxed, they immediately became calm and well; so that it seemed to be demonstrated before the eyes of the credulous audience that the malign miasm had been received back again into the witch.

She herself could not tell what to make of it, and never doubted the fact that the girls suffered as they seemed to do; she only declared that it was not she that caused it, and must be the others—which simple exclamation the justices used as a confession of her own guilt, and accusation and evidence against the others. "What is it that you say," asked Hathorne, "when you go muttering away from persons' houses?" "If I must tell, I will tell," she answers. "Do tell us, then," he urges.

THE LEGEND OF SALEM.

"THE REV. GEORGE BURROUGHS WAS ACCUSED OF WITCHCRAFT ON THE EVIDENCE OF FEATS OF STRENGTH, TRIED, HUNG, AND BURIED BENEATH THE GALLOWS."

George Burroughs standing in the courtroom during the Salem witch trials, his hands in chains. He was hung, and then buried beneath the gallows. Newspaper illustration from 1871.

justice was weak or non-existent. This was also evident in Scotland where judicial power and its reestablishment ended a particularly vicious hunt in 1597. Likewise in Spain new judicial instructions effectively brought a witch-hunt in the Basque country to an end in 1611. However even episodes like the Salem witch-hunt indicated that the legal tide was turning. Although nearly forty people died at Salem, it could have been much, much worse had the governor of the colony Sir William Phipps not striven to intervene. One factor that had persuaded him to do so was the growing scepticism of intellectuals and theologians. In particular Phipps had read a book by the influential writer Increase Mather. In this work, *Cases of Conscience*, Mather strongly criticised the use of spectral evidence and pushed the idea that rational evidence should be used to convict people accused of witchcraft rather than fear, presumption and suspicion. In this he famously declared that he would rather ten witches escape than a wholly innocent individual be punished. This attitude would have been totally alien to those in charge of the witch-hunt at Bamberg, where it was vital all witches should be eliminated irrespective of the level of meaningful proof against them, and demonstrates how cultural and legal attitudes to witchcraft had really begun to change. It is no surprise that some historians have linked changes in attitude to forms of belief and ideas as an important stage in producing a modern society with fundamentally different ideas about the universe and how it operated. However we might also listen to those who suggest witchcraft prosecutions effectively died out because of a growing reluctance to prosecute and convict.

The Wonders of the Invisible World:

Being an Account of the

T R Y A L S

OF

Several Witches,

Lately Executed in

NEW-ENGLAND:

And of several remarkable Curiosities therein Occurring.

Together with,

I. Observations upon the Nature, the Number, and the Operations of the Devils.
II. A short Narrative of a late outrage committed by a knot of Witches in Swedo-Land, very much resembling, and so far explaining, that under which New-England has laboured.
III. Some Councils directing a due Improvement of the Terrible things lately done by the unusual and amazing Range of Evil-Spirits in New-England.
IV. A brief Discourse upon those Temptations which are the more ordinary Devices of Satan.

By COTTON MATHER.

Published by the Special Command of his EXCELLENCY the Governour of the Province of the Massachusetts-Bay in New-England.

Printed first, at Boston in New-England; and Reprinted at London, for John Dunton, at the Raven in the Poultry. 1693.

Printed account of the trials of several witches executed in New England, by Cotton Mather, printed in 1693.

'The Trial of a Witch, seventeenth-century Puritan America', A nineteenth-century illustration for the play *Giles Corey, Yeoman* by Mary E. Wilkins.

THE AFTERLIFE OF WITCH-HUNTING

IT WOULD BE TEMPTING to try to locate a precise date for when the early modern witch-hunt came to an end, however history is rarely so neat and tidy. Certainly in England the statute of 1735 dramatically altered the law and the attitude of government and it is tempting to see this statute as really demonstrating how much had changed. Claiming to be a witch, and to undertake activities associated with this claim, was no longer a dangerous and heinous crime. Under this statute it became a species of fraud to make such a claim – indicating a new official attitude since such claims were now to be dismissed as fabrications. Nonetheless beliefs about witches, witchcraft and the Devil certainly did not vanish overnight. A useful way to think about how the old world and the new overlapped is provided by the occasion of the last ducking for witchcraft in England. Ducking – or the practice of 'swimming a witch' – had been largely pioneered by Matthew Hopkins in England. This was based on the belief that since witches were unnatural they would be actively rejected by natural phenomena in the world around us – thus water would 'reject' the witch. Hopkins sought permission from those accused to be ducked in a local pond or waterway. If they floated (or were visibly rejected by water) they would be considered guilty. However, if they sank and were swiftly retrieved then their innocence would be proven. The last ducking for witchcraft in England occurred in the year 1776 – the same year that the American colonists signed the Declaration of Independence on the other side of the Atlantic. The first of these indicates an old world reliant upon the persistence of pre-modern beliefs, whilst the second produced political ideas fundamental to the foundation of the modern world.

It is possible to suggest that the belief in witches belonged to an earlier period in the psychological and cultural development of Western society. Certainly this was the idea behind probably the largest and most comprehensive study of witchcraft beliefs in England – Keith Thomas's *Religion and the Decline of Magic* (1971). This idea was part of a theory that

Opposite:
Illustration of Hansel and Gretel and the witch by Arthur Rackham, from a 1909 translation of *The Fairy Tales of the Brothers Grimm*.

Trial of a witch by ducking in the millstream.

humans were undergoing a process of modernisation whereby rational explanations were increasingly coming to replace the irrational. Certainly it is possible to consider how advances in medicine and knowledge about the mechanisms that shaped the world may well have altered elite perceptions that had previously fostered the idea of witches and a diabolical presence in the universe. Sometimes the irrational ideas which produced persecution became associated with earlier, more extreme forms of religious zeal. Certainly in England, after the Restoration in 1660, hunting witches seemed a primitive symptom of a more barbarous period. However rather less is known about how all these changes had an impact upon the lives of the populace at large. Folk beliefs in rural and remote areas took some time to disappear and certainly survived long enough to be collected by folklorists in the nineteenth century and to make the occasional appearance in popular fiction such as Thomas Hardy's *Mayor of Casterbridge*.

One clear and unequivocal legacy of witch-hunting and witch beliefs can be found in the multitude of collections of folk and fairy tales, the collation of which was something of a hobby and obsession in the nineteenth century. Considered curios and forms of entertainment, such stories must have partly scared many generations of children and arguably some adults. Other aspects of witchcraft and witch beliefs would have survived as superstition and practices to protect vulnerable groups, or individuals during vulnerable times in their lives (childbirth, childhood, marriage and fertility, illness and death).

In some localities memories of witch trials exercised a deep and lasting hold over the imagination of individuals. As seen in the last chapter, our knowledge of Salem and the 1692 witch-hunt is quite comprehensive. This has led to a whole industry investigating and bringing knowledge and perception of the event to the public at large. The Salem witch-hunt was consumed by nineteenth-century scholars every bit as much as it can now be experienced on the Internet, or through following any of the numerous tourist trails that run from many corners of Salem Village.

In some respects witchcraft and witch beliefs might have remained interesting pieces of folklore and as merely the subject of academic curiosity

had it not been for developments in some intellectual disciplines in the first quarter of the twentieth century. From the end of the nineteenth century, the discipline of anthropology had been anxious to find common beliefs among ethnically similar people. One anthropologist, Sir James Fraser, believed he had found a common myth (of a king who had volunteered to sacrifice himself for the sake of his people), which could be traced throughout Europe. In the years after the First World War anthropologists grew even more interested in this idea. The First World War had been a catastrophe for Western civilisation, as it had placed nations and ethnic groups against one another in a life or death struggle for supremacy. In the years after this conflict – alongside initiatives like the League of Nations – anthropologists started to search for things that would explain why nations and ethnic groups were linked together in a common heritage, rather than ways in which they could be pulled apart by more modern ideas and antagonistic ideologies.

Part of this mission inspired one anthropologist, Margaret Murray, to look again at the evidence of sixteenth-century witch trials. From looking at her evidence Murray argued that the witches were not guilty of witchcraft as the authorities had argued, but instead were the survivors of a pre-Christian fertility cult earlier described by Fraser. These groups, so Murray

The Witch House, Salem photographed in 1901, the sign above the left door reads 'Ye Old Witch House Antiques', and over right door 'Witch House'. Salem was already making a name for itself as 'the witch city', and those interested in witchcraft continue to visit.

argued, had been tolerated throughout Europe until the coming of a more militant Christianity that was intolerant of rival religions. Thus the crusade against witchcraft and witches had been Christianity's construction of a dangerous enemy that had to be eliminated. The unfortunate victims of

'The witch of Wall Street', 1909 illustration from *Puck*. The image of the witch has widely adopted in popular culture and political satire.

Christianity, turned militant and unforgiving, were merely innocent worshippers of a very benign fertility cult.

Although these ideas were later discredited, largely because Murray was very selective in the evidence she quoted, they did have a far-reaching influence in one particular direction. Many have noted that intellectuals in Nazi Germany was very interested in the occult and the supernatural, and some of this spilled over into the investigation of witchcraft. Heinrich Himmler established a special SS unit to investigate the history of witch trials in Germany. In many respects this took inspiration from the ideas of Fraser and Murray, who had both produced indictments of Christianity. This fitted in very well with aspects of Nazi ideology that believed Christianity and its heritage had damaged and softened Germany. Searching through the archives to find numerous trials where Christianity had oppressed, tortured, banished and executed innocent German Aryan women became important to Nazi ideology.

In 1944, Helen Duncan was the last woman to be imprisoned under the British Witchcraft Act of 1735. It is interesting to note that she was found guilty under the section of the act covering 'fraudulent witchcraft'!

In the post-war years interest in witchcraft and witches leaked into the cultural mainstream in the novels of writers such as Dennis Wheatley and built on the intellectual reputation of other writers associated with the occult, such as Aleister Crowley. Witches were very useful personifications of evil and were integral to a number of Hollywood films – such as the *Wizard of Oz* and *The Witches of Eastwick* – and several from the stable of 'Hammer' films produced in Britain. The new millennium has seen a significant upsurge of interest in the concept of the witch, displayed in books and films such as the *Harry Potter* series.

However there have also been other manifestations of interest in witchcraft and witches in other forms of popular culture. Some groups and individuals have now taken small sections of the wider conception of witchcraft and turned them into more modern beliefs or part-beliefs. This is very much a new phenomenon and many of these groups themselves recognise that they do not have any direct connection with witchcraft and witches of the early modern period. Some dissatisfaction with Christianity and its authority structures has led some to adopt aspects of what is now called Wicca. For some women Christianity's attitude to their status and sexuality has made these alternative choices rather more attractive, and they are seen as part of a genuinely feminist option. A similar stance has also been part of some brands of heavy metal

The Wicked Witch of the West melting after being doused with water by Dorothy. An illustration from the first edition of *The Wizard of Oz*.

Ceremony at Chalice Well during the 2009 Goddess Conference Glastonbury, Somerset.

The 1996 film *The Crucible* was based on Arthur Miller's play of the same name, centred on the Salem trials. The play, which opened on Broadway in 1953, was written as a parable of the Communist witch-hunts.

music, which has led to incendiary assaults on churches in Scandinavian countries. Likewise alternatives to systems of Western medicine have made the herbalists and their work – often associated with witchcraft – of greater importance in the contemporary world. This is not always a challenge to conventional medicine but instead is often evidence of choice being made available. Some aromatherapy oils, for example, are sold today with labels giving both a rational explanation of how they work on pain centres of the brain alongside a less rational explanation that individuals absorb the life force of the plants involved; the purchaser is offered the choice to believe a rational or non-rational explanation – neither of them is seen as pre-eminent or triumphant.

Academic interest in the subject was especially revived with the post-Second World War interest in social history. This meant stepping away from history's more traditional forms in favour of writing the history of those at the bottom of society and their experiences. This history-from-below approach made the social phenomena of witchcraft and witch-hunting of growing interest. It could not only teach historians about economic and social change, about economic and social tension and the impact of ideas and beliefs on people's lives, but also demonstrated how the law and attitudes of authority could literally spell the difference

between life and death for individuals. Historians have produced a range of studies on the history of witchcraft in individual countries but equally sometimes in regions (the study of the German witch-hunt examples has to adopt this approach for obvious reasons). Some historians investigate specific witch-hunts for which abundant records survive (e.g. the Salem witch-hunt of 1692). More recent work has led to many historians looking closely at some of the peripheral areas (such as Scandinavia, Russia, Poland and the Balkans) for new insights and comparative dimension to set beside what is known about the central European witch-hunts. Likewise new disciplines such as psychology and neuroscience are becoming involved in the study of the subject.

Whilst it is tempting to conclude that the history of witch beliefs, witchcraft and witch-hunting belongs to a remote and barbarous episode that mercifully ended with the coming of the Age of Enlightenment, the truth is rather more complex. It would be doing early modern people a disservice if we did not also recognise that many of them were actively sceptical about the reality of witches as a threat to Western human civilisation. Indeed the growing clamour of pamphlets from theologians expressing doubts and even ridiculing the belief in witchcraft changed the intellectual climate even before the Age of Enlightenment. Nonetheless this scepticism was not always total and could reflect distaste for one part of the collection of witch beliefs. This climate was only fatal to witch beliefs when combined with social and cultural change. Likewise it would be foolish to consider that irrational beliefs are wholly a thing of the past. Superstition, for example, still exerts a powerful hold over the human mind and becomes evident when individuals are under pressure or conceive themselves to be in many different types of danger. We need only look at the behaviour of sportsmen and -women to see how superstition is a central and important part of enabling them to compete to their best ability. One football club in the recent past was led to believe that a gypsy's curse had been placed on one end of their home ground. The officials of the club decided to have an exorcism to remove the curse on the grounds that doing so could do no harm and would only benefit the attitude of mind of the team's players. Thus an understanding of the apparently remote history of witchcraft can so easily become an understanding of a part of ourselves.

A cast-iron wall fountain in Edinburgh commemorating over three hundred women who were burned at the stake accused of being witches. In the sixteenth century more witch burnings were carried out at Castle Hill than anywhere else in Britain. The victims often suffered brutal torture before being put to death at the stake. They were often nearly drowned by being 'douked' in the Nor Loch (now Princes Street Gardens).

Statue of Alice Nutter, one of the Pendle witches, in her home village on Blacko Bar Road, Roughlee, Lancashire.

PLACES TO VISIT

The Museum of Witchcraft, The Harbour, Boscastle,
  Cornwall, PL35 0HD. Tel: 01840 250111.
  Website: www.museumofwitchcraft.com/contact_mow.php
Pendle Witches Trail. Website: www.visitlancashire.com/inspire-me/pendle-
  witches/on-the-trail-of-the-pendle-witches
Commemorating the life and death of ten witches executed in Lancashire
  in 1612.
Edinburgh Dungeon, 31 Market Street, Edinburgh,
  City of Edinburgh, EH1 1QB. Tel: 0871 423 2250.
  Website: www.thedungeons.com/edinburgh/en/
Covers the dungeon's whole history including the trial and execution
  of Scottish witches.
Salem Witch Museum, Washington Square, Salem, Massachusetts, USA. Tel:
  01970 978 744 1692. Website: www.salemwitchmuseum.com/
See also www.salemweb.com/guide/tosee.php for a general guide to the
  tourist opportunities in Salem, Massachusetts. This includes two other
  museums, a witch's house and other 'shows' and walks.
Museum of Torture, Oberstrasse 49-51, D-65385, Rudesheim, Germany. Tel:
  +49 (0) 6722/4 75 10. Website: www.foltermuseum.com/index_us.html
  This museum has material on the torture and execution of witches in early
  modern Germany.
Museum of Witchcraft Switzerland – Hexenmuseum Schweiz,
  Mühliacherweg 10 PO Box 22 5105 Auenstein. Tel: 062 897 39 09.
  Website: www.hexenmuseum.ch/rechtshinweis.htm

FURTHER READING

Ankarloo, Bengt and Henningsen, Gustav (eds.). *Early Modern European Witchcraft: Centres and Peripheries* (Oxford: Clarendon, 1989).

Clark, Stuart. *Languages of Witchcraft: Narrative, Ideology, and Meaning in Early Modern Culture* (Basingstoke: Macmillan, 2001).

Davies, Owen. *Beyond the Witch Trials: Witchcraft and Magic in Enlightenment Europe* (Manchester/New York: Manchester University Press, 2004).

Gibson, Marion. *Reading Witchcraft: Stories of Early English Witches* (London/New York, 1999).

Goodare, Julian. *The Scottish Witch-Hunt in Context* (Manchester: Manchester University Press, 2002).

Larner, Christina. *Enemies of God: The Witch-Hunt in Scotland* (Baltimore: Johns Hopkins University Press, 1981).

Levack, Brian (ed.). *The Oxford Handbook of Witchcraft* (Oxford, 2013).

Levack, Brian. *The Witch-Hunt in Early Modern Europe (3rd edition)* (London, 2006,).

Macfarlane, Alan. *Witchcraft in Tudor and Stuart England: A Regional and Comparative Study* (London: Routledge, 1999).

Maxwell-Stuart, P. G. *Witchcraft in Europe and the New World, 1400–1800* (Basingstoke/New York: Palgrave, 2001).

Roper, Lyndal. *Oedipus and the Devil: Witchcraft, Sexuality and Religion in Early Modern Europe* (London/New York: Routledge, 1994).

Scarre, Geoffrey and Callow, John. *Witchcraft and Magic in Sixteenth- and Seventeenth-Century Europe, Studies in European History (2nd edition)* (Basingstoke: Palgrave Macmillan, 2001).

Sharpe, J. A. *The Bewitching of Anne Gunter: A Horrible and True Story of Football, Witchcraft, Murder and the King of England* (London: Profile, 1999).

Sharpe, J. A. *Instruments of Darkness: Witchcraft in England 1550–1750* (London/New York: Hamish Hamilton/Penguin, 1996).

Thomas, Keith. *Religion and the Decline of Magic: Studies in Popular Beliefs in Sixteenth- and Seventeenth-Century England* (Harmondsworth: Peregrine Books, 1978).

Thurston, Robert W. *Witch, Wicce, Mother Goose: The Rise and Fall of the Witch Hunts in Europe and North America* (Harlow: Longman 2001).

Stone commemorating the death of Giles Corey, pressed to death during the Salem witch trials. The stone forms part of the Tricentennial Memorial.

INDEX